I0158138

THE BIRDS ARE STILL SINGING IN POMPEII

ESSAYS TO MY GRANDDAUGHTER RACHEL

Selina Inabinet Duncan

Copyright 2012 by Selina Inabinet Duncan
No part of this book may be reproduced in any manner
whatsoever without the express written permission of
the copyright holder.

ISBN: 978-0936497631
Seven Worlds Corporation
1004 Reunion Drive
Chattanooga, TN 37421

For more Seven Worlds Books please got to
www.sevenworldspub.com

SEVEN WORLDS

PUBLISHING

DEDICATION

To my husband, **King**, *who taught me to see the possibilities and who believes in me. Love and thanks . . .*

To my four daughters and sons-in-law: **Rebecca** *and* **Stephen Clark**, **Deborah** *and* **Greg Hyde**, **Angela** *and* **Bill Akers**, *and* **Selina Duncan** *(Jr.) and* **Christian Horvath**. *You live out the wisdom in these essays. Thank you for loving me and making me a better person because of it.*

To my OTHER grandchildren: **Sebastian**, **Anna** *and* **Luka**. *You know Grandmama's heart by now, so you know that these words are meant for you as well. Know how much I love you . . .*

INTRODUCTION

Twenty-two years old . . . how can you be twenty-two already? I was there when you were born, and twenty-two years haven't passed for me. Well, maybe they have . . . so, it's about time I told you some things I think it's important to know to get along in this old world.

The essay format seems a useful device to employ to impart my thoughts-in-progress to you. Sixteenth-century French writer Michel Eyquem de Montaigne developed this method, a sort of candid informality, from the French verb *essayer*, meaning "to try." "Montaigne meant to sort through his life as truthfully as possible and to *try* to understand himself and his world as he went along, without coming to any final conclusions."[1]

In my essays to you, I won't come to any final conclusions either, because, in the long run, you are the one who chooses to sew the stitches that become your tapestry of life. And, perhaps, your tapestry will be much more beautiful than I could ever envision. In these essays I'll give you a little bit of me, a little bit of my limited grandmotherly wisdom culled from sixty-seven years of living, interspersed with lots of quotes from other wiser sages. That's why you'll see footnotes scattered around these essays.

Imagine being a person of Jewish descent living in Poland in the 1930s. Nazi forces are advancing across Europe. Jews are being rounded up and arrested. Their possessions are confiscated, their homes destroyed. Most Jewish people are sent to concentration camps, where they face beatings, torture, forced labor, starvation, and mass executions.

Many of these Jewish people coped with their losses by writing what has been called "ethical wills." Because they no longer had anything of material value to bequeath to future generations, they wrote wills stating who they were, what they valued most in life, and the values they wanted to pass on to their children and grandchildren. Many of these ethical wills were stored in a synagogue basement, where they were discovered after the war.[2]

If I were writing an ethical will to you, Rachel, these essays contain some of the values I want to pass on to you.

All your teachers have told you to prepare an outline before you start your paper, so here's an outline of my essays to you:

Essay I –   *Develop your sense of wonder*
Essay II –   *Believe in yourself*
Essay III –   *Learn from your mistakes*
Essay IV –   *Love unconditionally*
Essay V –   *Change the world*

I. DEVELOP YOUR SENSE OF WONDER

I like to call wonder being "serendipitously surprised by the common." How many times have you seen a flower push its way through the cracks of a concrete sidewalk and said, "Wow, how can that happen? I know that a flower does not have the strength to do that, but there it is!" How many times have you listened to a piece of music and felt in your inner being the movement and rhythm that suddenly made your soul soar? Or read a moving piece that caused tears to flow and your heart to skip a beat? You say, "Wow! Wow! How awesome!

I was in the Louvre in Paris looking at all the wondrous art work, pieces that I had only read about before. I was struck by paintings and sculptures that pierced my memory from books, and suddenly I walked into one of the galleries and saw at a distance the painting "Mona Lisa" by Leonardo Da Vinci. Even standing far away from it, I was amazed by its beauty and overtaken by a sense of awe and started crying.

Crying in the Louvre—crying because of the wonder of being surrounded by these masterpieces, awe because I was in the presence of artists through the centuries who had no limitation to their imaginations, who saw the magnificent image in the marble while it was yet untouched.

Rachel, this is what I want for you: that you cultivate your sense of wonder, that you look for the "awe" in life. It will bring you so much joy.

A long while back I read an article by Arthur Gordon concerning this. He recalled a conversation he had with the psychiatrist Smiley Blanton. Dr. Blanton said that we have a sixth sense. "It's the capacity," he said, "to feel wonder. The five other senses bring knowledge, and knowledge improves the mind. But wonder expands the soul."

Dr. Blanton goes on to say, "I know when I feel it, and so do you. Children come into this world trailing clouds of it, but too often as they grow older it fades away. All of us live surrounded by incredible marvels, but gradually we begin to take them for granted—unless we train ourselves to look through the prism of wonder."[3]

Consider the characteristics of a child: exuberance, expectation, excitement, naiveté, openness, and acceptance. Remember that children trail clouds of wonder. What do children do to experience wonder? They keep the door of their heart open in anticipation of wonderful things they will experience in life. Rachel, I hope you will keep the door of YOUR HEART open also.

What wonder does for us:

1. Wonder helps us see ourselves in relation to the whole. We realize that there is overpowering grandeur all around us, but that WE ARE PART OF IT ALL! We fit in. I've always marveled at the abundant generosity of nature. Consider how every tree has different leaves.

In middle school (it was called Junior High then!) I had to do a "Leaf Notebook" for one of my classes. The goal was to find as many different species of leaves as you could, identify and categorize them, and put them in a notebook. What I learned is that different trees produce leaves that are structured differently; the blade, stem, and veins are varied. And think of the number and variety of birds that inhabit our earth—and the beauty of them! And did you know that there are 7,500 varieties of apples?

Think of the people you know—their personalities, their colors, their abilities and skills. How abundant, how grand! And how we, as human beings, move, breathe, live and thrive in this generosity!

2. Wonder makes us humble—not in a self-effacing way, but in a healthy, balanced way. Truly humble people seem to have a great sense of awareness, of self-understanding. They exude a quiet confidence that causes them to value human life but not judge people. They treat old and young alike, they listen, they seem more wise and trustworthy. Humble people have a greater sense of peace because they take the focus off themselves and, in turn, demonstrate compassion to others.

3. Wonder makes us grateful. Rachel, if you added up all the things you're grateful for, how long would that list be? When you look around at the vastness of our universe, and the beauty of it, of the kindness of other people, of the opportunities for growth and learning, of your unlimited possibilities—surely your heart swells with gratitude!

A person with a grateful heart experiences freedom; an "attitude of gratitude" cleanses the soul. It flushes out negativity so that we can see beauty in everyday life. And gratitude leads to contentment and this contentment leads to inner peace and joy.

There is an old legend about discouragement. It seems that the seeds of discouragement can grow anywhere, profusely and abundantly. According to this legend, the only place the seeds of discouragement cannot grow is in the heart of a grateful person.

Dr. Joyce Brothers said: Count up everything you're grateful for, including your own talents, and then "gratitude—the mighty river to happiness—begins its journey through your soul."[4]

Rachel, I firmly believe that when you experience wonder in life, you become respectful of the awe-some-ness of life and living, and then you will have an inner serenity that will transcend daily stumbling blocks. Looking for and finding wonder in your life does not guarantee that problems will be solved and rainbows will miraculously appear in the sky, but it does guarantee that you'll have joy in your life. "A bird does not sing because it has an answer. It sings because it has a song." (Chinese proverb)

There will be a thing called "Hope" that will nestle in your being and cause you to touch your power and soar; you will know your strength and personal effectiveness. Now, what is this thing called Hope?

You're familiar with the Greek myth of Pandora. Pandora was given a box by the gods, but told never to open it. Her curiosity got the better of her and she did open the box. Out came plagues and swarms of evil, and she immediately shut the box, but not in time. The world was overcome with all these evils. One thing remained in the box and Pandora lifted the lid to release it. This one good thing was HOPE, and it now remains to comfort and encourage humanity.

What I want to say to you is that wonder paves the way to hope, and hope is all about the future.

Granddad and I had the privilege of going to Italy a few years back. It was a wonderful trip—the sights of Rome, Naples, Pisa, Venice, Milan. Boy, let me tell you, you can't keep them down on the farm when they've seen Italy!

Near Naples is the ancient ruined city of Pompeii. It was destroyed in 79 AD by the eruption of the volcano Vesuvius. We walked through the ruins with our guide map, which showed the streets of Pompeii, where the buildings and shops and homes used to be.

There we were getting our shoes strangely dirtied in the volcanic ash of 2,000 years ago, imagining rooms that used to be, in a city dead for hundreds of years. "A dead city," I thought to myself with sadness. How bleak, how nothing . . . how absolutely nothing.

Then, suddenly, I heard a bird singing. Looking around, I saw it perched on the chipped and dusty corner of one of the buildings. My ears opened, my heart opened, my soul opened! How extraordinary to hear beauty of that magnitude in a place of destruction!

The bird's song soared and dipped, and with every note, that thing, that intangible thing, that indomitable spirit, that will to live, and live fully arose within me. If a bird can sing amidst the ashes of death, how can I deny that vestige of soul that cries out in hope and joy that I, too, can sing!

I coined a phrase that spoke to me of hope: The Birds are Still Singing in Pompeii. In the devastation of an ancient city overcome by volcanic ash, the birds are still singing. Hope addresses the future head on.

Rachel, in your times of trouble and living in your Pompeii, I wish for you that the birds will continue to sing and bring you hope. As someone once said:

Hope looks for the good in people, instead of harping on the worst.

Hope opens doors where despair closes them.

Hope discovers what can be done, instead of grumbling about what cannot.

Hope draws its power from a deep trust in God, and in the basic goodness of humankind.

Hope lights a candle, instead of cursing the darkness.

Hope regards problems, small or large, as opportunities.

Hope sets big goals and is not frustrated by repeated difficulties or setbacks.

Hope accepts misunderstanding as the price for serving the greater good of others . . .

(James Keller)

Remember that wonder paves the way for hope, and hope looks to the future, because hope knows that it can overcome and conquer ANYTHING.

"A bird does not sing because it has an answer. It sings because it has a song." – Chinese proverb

II. BELIEVE IN YOURSELF

Rachel, there is a sentence in "Desiderata" that has had meaning for me through the years: "You are a child of the universe no less than the trees and the stars; you have a right to be here." (Max Ehrmann)

I take that to mean that the essence of us—our self—is precious, important in the scheme of things. In order for you to believe in yourself, you must **KNOW THAT YOU ARE LOVED**. How many times have I written to you and ended my letter with, "Know how much I love you." Too numerous to count! But it's so important that you look back over your life and remember the times that family and friends have been there for you, expressing love to you through myriad acts of kindness and concern.

Years ago, when I was pregnant with your mother and living hundreds of miles away from home, my mother sent me a care package to help me through the pregnancy. It contained the standard items: maternity clothes, maternity underwear, a letter with some gems of advice, blank thank-you notes (expected for that era!), and then, in the bottom of the package there was a pair of fancy, high-heeled bedroom slippers. Satiney white with cut-out toes and fluffy pom-poms and rhinestones on the top. I couldn't wear high-heels at that time in life (I was already as big as an elephant—or so I thought!). But those slippers were beautiful!

My mother said to me, with that gesture, that I was loved. To give me a wonderfully frivolous and exquisite gift like that told me that she believed in me, believed that one day I wouldn't look like an elephant, that maybe, maybe, I'd be a pretty good mother after all. She loved me!

Your grandparents and aunts and uncles recall your earlier years with affection. How you graced everyone with your drawings, how you have music and dance in every fiber of your body, and how you express love to all you meet. It is reciprocated, Rachel, you are loved.

VALUE YOURSELF. Another aspect of believing in yourself is being satisfied with who you are and knowing that you matter in life. I've enjoyed reading

The Book of Abigail and John, which contains letters that Abigail and John Adams wrote to each other during the years of 1762 to 1784. These letters were written during the tumultuous time when the U.S. was breaking away from Great Britain.

Consistently Abigail Adams expressed her opinions to her husband about managing the farm, the dignity of women, raising their children, intricate details about public policy and matters of diplomacy. "She hardly knew how to write a dull paragraph. Signed or unsigned, her letters bear the unmistakable marks of her perceptiveness, her total self-possession, and her artless but captivating personal style. . . . That her political opinions were usually formed independently rather than absorbed from her husband is indicated by her frequently anticipating him."[5] Even in the 1700s Abigail Adams knew who she was and that she mattered in life.

Now, being satisfied with who you are takes into consideration your appearance. But make no mistake about it, I mean your INNER APPEARANCE, for inner beauty is infinitely more important than outer beauty. There is dignity and preciousness in every human being. C. S. Lewis said, "We are not ordinary mortals, but everlasting splendors." So the goal is to create within yourself an inner beauty that gives a serenity and a glow to your soul.

Nell Mohney defines several characteristics that are part of your inner beauty: integrity, compassion, cheerfulness, being nonjudgmental, and the ability to laugh at yourself. If these five characteristics are part of your life, Rachel, you will truly be beautiful.

You value yourself and create that inner beauty by **developing a character that is worthy of respect**. You develop that character by making the right choices at those pivotal moments in life when your integrity is on the line.

A person with character worthy of respect knows to hold onto her core values. You know, Rachel, we define who we are in the course of our travel through time. We go through stages of life, and those stages are not stagnant; they're forever changing and flowing. It's crucial that we center ourselves in the basic values we learned in our home life and in our places of worship so that when change comes in the form of new events, emotional upsets, challenges and problems, we return to our core.

A person of character knows to evaluate new theories and new innovations in the light of their values, to use their sieve of discernment to hold on to that which counts and let go of that which is destructive. We hold to what is basic, what is fundamental, what is "right" as we understand it.

Another way to believe in yourself is to **PRACTICE POSITIVE SELF TALK**. Life Studies Institute concluded a study that indicated that by the age of sixteen the average person receives 173,000 negative messages about themselves (29.6 per day). On the other hand, the same person will receive 16,000 positive messages about themselves (2.7 per day).

What that says to me, Rachel, is that we'd better say good and worthy things to ourselves because others certainly aren't doing it! The words we use have a tremendous effect on our thought processes. "I can't, I'm afraid, it won't work, it's no use"—words like these drag us down mentally and physically. You know how Granddaddy occasionally calls your cousin Luka, Luka "I Can" Hyde. Well, that's to help him understand that he can accomplish anything.

When you use self talk you're talking to your mind. It's something you do all your waking hours. Your mind is constantly thinking, so it's important to fill it with affirmations. Being aware of what you're thinking and, if needed, changing those thoughts to positive self talk is essential.

> Watch your thoughts, for they become words.
> Watch your words, for they become actions.
> Watch your actions, for they become habits.
> Watch your habits, for they become character.
> Watch your character, for it becomes your destiny.
> (Frank Outlaw)

Believing in yourself also demands that you **PRACTICE SELF-CONTROL**. It calls for discipline of body, soul and mind so that your choices always reflect your better self: that self that has high morals, compassion for others, a sense of rightness that comes from a measured weighing of the pros and cons of a situation and then determining the most appropriate outcome.

Alfred, Lord Tennyson once said, "Self-reverence, self-knowledge, self-control—these three alone lead to power." And yes, Rachel, there is power in keeping your behavior, emotions, speech and all other aspects of your life under control. This power banishes fear and infuses you with strength.

You've probably heard about the marshmallow test. In 1972, in an experiment at Stanford University day care, psychologist Walter Mischel placed 4-year-olds alone in a room with a marshmallow. He told them they could eat the marshmallow now or wait and be given two marshmallows later. Some of the children ate the one marshmallow right away, but some, through various methods of self-control, waited so they could have the reward of two marshmallows.

Well, the surprising result of this study came almost two decades later. It was found that those children who practiced self-control with the marshmallows performed much better in life later on; they were psychologically well adjusted, dependable and scored higher on their SATs.[6]

And, since I'm on a roll with "self" words, the last thing that is important for you to Believe In Yourself is **SELF-ESTEEM**. Let me try to create a definition of what I mean by self-esteem. Maybe it would be best to say what self-esteem is not. It's not narcissistic, it's not self-serving, it's not believing that you're better than others. What it is is a belief that you are capable (have the ability, the means by force of mind and body) to solve problems that come your way.

It also means that you have a right to happiness in your life. Self-esteem knows that you are equal to others and also recognizes and respects the differences in others.

As your granddaddy says in his book, *The Amazing Law of Influence*, "Self-esteem means so many things. It means getting along comfortably with other people and forming lasting, mature relationships. It means living from day to day without feelings of guilt, fear or regret. It means courage in the face of adversity or change, and the ability to take charge when others are afraid to do so. Self-esteem means avoiding self-destructive behaviors and actions that cause others pain. It results in openness and sharing, respect for others and genuine benevolence."[7]

Persons with high self-esteem naturally want to help others. They've gotten beyond the self-absorbed me-me attitude to the knowledge that they're comfortable with themselves and can now reach out to others to meet their needs.

I want to end this essay—Believe in Yourself— with a story about a tradition of an East African tribe. When a baby is on the way, the mother goes off alone and spends time listening until she hears her baby's "song." This song celebrates the uniqueness of that child. She comes back to the village and teaches the song to her husband. They sing it together over and over until time for the baby to be born, then they teach it to the midwives and they, in turn, sing it during the birth.

This same melodic and distinctive song is sung for every celebration of that person's life—puberty, graduation, marriage—until that person dies. And it is sung one last time upon his death. That song is never sung again because it belonged to that precious one-of-a-kind individual.[8]

You have a song, Rachel, a deep and beautiful song that identifies who you are. It encompasses all your lovely attributes and speaks of a magnificent future for you. It is yours and yours alone. So sing YOUR SONG as you go through this journey called life. Don't even attempt to sing anyone else's song. Yours was made for you. You are unique and wondrously made—Believe in Yourself!

III.   LEARN FROM YOUR MISTAKES

Rachel, if I were to pen a subtitle for this third essay, it would be "On Not Having To Look Over Your Shoulder." What do I mean by that? The gist of what I want to express in this essay is this:

It's important in life that you're honest, that you walk the talk, that you align your behavior with the inherent "ought-tos" you've been taught so that the end result is peace of mind—not having to look over your shoulder hoping no one will find out you've cheated, you're dishonest, you're lacking in integrity.

Everybody makes mistakes; it's part of being human. When you live an active and full life, mistakes are bound to happen. Choices you make at a moment of weakness regurgitate, and spill over into every aspect of life. These choices come back to haunt you years and years later. How you deal with them will shape your character. I have some grandmotherly suggestions for dealing with life's mistakes:

1. ACKNOWLEDGE YOUR MISTAKES. Own up to them. Only then will you be able to see your way to a solution. Polish writer Stanislaw Lec said, "Each snowflake in an avalanche pleads not guilty." But the truth is, you ARE responsible for all of your actions, no one else. He/she "made" me do it is no excuse.

On lying: "One little lie can't hurt. But a lie never stays outside of us. It enters our hearts. It penetrates our minds. It invades our souls. It takes away the simplicity of our characters, our forthrightness, our integrity. It takes away the grace of truth in us, and it makes us cunning and false. Not that we tell a lie, but that we become a liar. Not that we utter a falsehood, but that we become false. And our courage is lost with our integrity."[9]

On gossip:
Once I tarnish a reputation, it is never the same.
I topple governments and wreck marriages.
I ruin careers and cause sleepless nights, heartaches and indigestion.
I make innocent people cry into their pillows.
Even my name hisses. I am called Gossip.
-- Author unknown

2. FORGIVE YOURSELF. All too often we allow ourselves to be overwhelmed by our mistakes, and we lose our perspective. We think to ourselves that it is the end of the world. But it isn't. Tomorrow the sun is going to rise again. Somewhere birds will sing and flowers will bloom. You will still have food to eat and clothes to wear, and you will be able to continue with your life. Ralph Waldo Emerson said:

> Finish each day and be done with it.
> You have done what you could;
> Some blunders and absurdities no doubt crept in
> Forget them as soon as you can
> Tomorrow is a new day;
> You shall begin it well and serenely . . .

Rachel, as painful as mistakes and failures are, if you face up to them, you always grow from these difficulties. Yes, it's a moment of judgment for you, but it's also a moment of opportunity. This is where the mettle of your character emerges. As you ask forgiveness, as you make amends, as you right a wrong, you reorient your life to encompass a sensitive conscience and an inner peace. "If you have made mistakes . . . there is always another chance for you . . . you may have a fresh start any moment you choose, for this thing we call 'failure' is not the falling down, but the staying down."[10]

To rise again with renewed integrity, humility and kindness toward others is your goal. Never be afraid to take on new challenges because of a mistake you made in the past; you'll be better equipped to handle challenges because of the lessons you've learned. In defeat, you'll rise to greater service to humanity, your tears of shame will spur you to compassion, your agony will produce hope. In the words of George Roemisch:

> Forgiveness is the fragrance of the violet which still clings fast to the
> heel that crushed it.
> Forgiveness is the broken dream which hides itself within the corner of the mind
> oft called forgetfulness so that it will not bring pain to the dreamer.
> Forgiveness is the reed which stands up straight and green
> when nature's mighty rampage halts, full speed.
> Forgiveness is a God who will not leave us
> after all we've done.[11]

3. ASK FOR HELP. "The healthy and strong individual is the one who asks for help when he needs it. Whether he's got an abscess on his knee or in his soul."[12]

No truer words are spoken, especially when you've made a mistake. Ask someone wiser, more grounded in strength of character, someone who has a serenity about them that has come from their mistakes overcome. It is a difficult thing to confess your sins, but so freeing. You can deal with the abscess on your knee, but you need help to deal with the abscess in your soul.

4. KNOW WHAT TO CHANGE. Wouldn't it be great if we had the good sense and force of will that Benjamin Franklin had when he analyzed his life and determined virtues that he wished to attain? In his *Autobiography* he states thirteen admirable virtues that he would systematically work on. His method was to write these virtues in a notebook, spend one week diligently pursuing each virtue, and by force of habit his life would change for the better. His belief was that habits modified human behavior. Now, how do you change to acquire better habits?

Recognize that change requires a 180 degree position readjustment. A person can't expect to change if she doesn't appreciate a cause and effect dimension to her behavior. I like what Dietrich Bonhoeffer said about this: "If you board the wrong train, it is no use running along the corridor in the other direction." You're still on the wrong train!

Rachel, only you know what needs to change in your life, but keep this in mind: there is beauty in goodness. I said at the beginning of this essay that the wrong things we do come back to haunt us years and years later.

My mother, your great-grandmother whom you called Nabby, was an expert seamstress. She taught me that when you're cutting cloth with scissors, if you look only at the point of the cut while using the scissors, you end up with a jagged and uneven line. Nabby said to look ahead to the end of the fabric to achieve the precision of your cut.

You will someday get to the end of your life; I truly hope it will be a long, long line. But it's those jagged and uneven lines—those behaviors that are wrong, those bad decisions, those insensitive acts—that cause our conscience to be unsettled and eat at our happiness. In life, look ahead so that you live a life that is straight.

IV. LOVE UNCONDITIONALLY

People are often unreasonable, illogical and self-centered;
Forgive them anyway.

If you are kind, people may accuse you of selfish, ulterior motives;
Be kind anyway.

If you're successful, you will win some unfaithful friends and some genuine enemies;
Succeed anyway.

If you are honest and sincere, people may deceive you;
Be honest and sincere anyway.

What you spend years creating, others could destroy overnight;
Create anyway.

If you find serenity and happiness, they may be jealous;
Be happy anyway.
The good you do today, will often be forgotten;
Do good anyway.
Give the world the best you have, and it will never be enough;
Give your best anyway.
In the final analysis, it is between you and God;
It was never between you and them anyway.[13]

Rachel, this fourth essay is possibly the hardest to write. We sing "Love Makes the World Go 'Round," and, yes, love does define and encompass almost everything we are and do. But it is so hard to go beyond just the love part to the unconditional part. The poem above gives us a clue to what the picture of unconditional love looks like.

But first, maybe it would help for me to tell you **what I know about love:**

1. Love is not something you fall into; you work at it.

2. Love is about commitment and principles. Love is a choice; you choose to love and that brings responsibility.

3. Love doesn't protect us from life's tragedies.

4. Love gives us motivation for living and hope for tomorrow.

5. Love is more important than winning.

6. Love keeps on giving. The more you love, the more you have love to give.

7. Love makes us bold, takes fear from our hearts.

8. Love has no tally sheet.

9. Love is patient and kind.

10. Love never ends.

Now, the next question is: **How do you love unconditionally**? The definition of unconditional is "absolute, without qualifying conditions." True unreserved love assumes that you'll be a moral person.

You can't live an immoral life and love others, because immorality begins from a premise of selfishness. Immoral people look only to themselves; they have no regard for others. Rachel, I truly believe that we are obligated to love, that when we cease to love, we cease being human.

I believe that three things have to happen for unconditional love to become a reality. First, you have to **respect** every person. Second, you will experience **sacrifice** to love unconditionally. And third, you have to **act** of your own volition to extend love unconditionally.

1. RESPECT – Samuel Taylor Coleridge said: "Trample not on any; there may be some work of grace there, that thou knowest not of." It's easy to love those who are like us: people who have the same values, like the same music, are of the same temperament, believe as we believe and move in the same social circle.

In southern Africa, the Bebemba tribe has a fascinating procedure for combating feelings of rejection and wrongdoing in their tribe. Each person in the tribe who acts irresponsibly or unjustly is taken alone to the center of the village. Everyone in the village stops work and gathers in a large circle around the accused. In turn, each person in the tribe—regardless of age—speaks to the individual, recounting aloud the good things he has done in his lifetime.

All the positive incidents in the person's life, plus his good attributes, strengths, and kindnesses, are recalled with accurate detail. Not one word about his irresponsible or antisocial behavior is shared.

The ceremony, which sometimes lasts for several days, isn't complete until every positive expression has been given by those assembled. At the conclusion of the ceremony, the person is welcomed back into the tribe.[14]

The Bebemba tribe shows us how to respect others: love and accept others with joy in spite of their flaws; in others see no sin, make no judgment, see only a soul.

2. SACRIFICE – Unconditional love knows that some people are wounded emotionally. They need pure love. Give it to them. So many people are lonely, emotionally crippled, so lacking in self-esteem— unconditional love is what they seek and need. Love people who are the least lovable, because they need it the most.

Unconditional love knows that some people are wounded physically; they need love especially. Give it to them.

Irish poet Thomas Moore had a beautiful wife whom he loved dearly. He was called away for a length of time, and during that period, his wife contracted smallpox. No medicine cured it at that time, and those who survived developed horrible scars and sores. Mrs. Moore was no exception.

After recovering she shut herself up in her darkened room and refused to see anyone. Thomas returned and went to his wife's room. She yelled to him: "No, Thomas! Come no nearer! I have resolved that you will never again see me by the light of day!"

That night Thomas Moore wrote these lines to his wife:

Believe me, if all those endearing young charms,
Which I gaze on so fondly today,
Were to change by tomorrow and flee from my arms,
Like fairy gifts fading away,
Thou would'st still be adored, as this moment thou art.
Let thy loveliness fade as it will;
And around the dear ruin each wish of my heart
Would entwine itself verdantly still.

At the first ray of sunshine the next morning, Thomas read this verse to his wife and kissed her disfigured face, and she fell into his arms. So greatly did she experience unconditional love![15]

3. ACT – Unconditional love seeks those who need it; it's a proactive effort on your part to step beyond your comfort zone, to seek out all those who need unconditional love and to fight the barriers they erect to receiving that love. It is to love the ugly—in behavior, appearance and spirit—so that they come round to knowing that they too are persons of dignity, worth and beauty.

Every person has inherent value no matter what circumstances they're in: poverty or wealth, health or illness, mental anguish or peaceful repose. Seek out everyone who needs your unconditional love. Greek philosopher Euripides said: "Love is all we have, the only way that each can help the other."

This love walks, talks and serves others. It makes a difference in our own lives, and it makes a profound difference in the world. I like what Madeleine L'Engle said about it: ". . . everything in Creation affects the whole. If we are willing to contemplate all that is around us, to love it, to help make it real, we are adding to the health and beauty and reality of the entire universe."[16]

V. CHANGE THE WORLD

Rachel, this final—yes, final!—essay is titled, "You Can Change the World." What I mean by that is that you have a responsibility, as everyone else does, to consciously seek out ways to improve our world.

Sidney Poitier was asked what he wanted to leave his great-granddaughter, and he said, "I want her to know that the responsibility for the survival of the human family rests exclusively on the human family—and that she needs to be part of the energy that will contribute to that survival."[17]

Because you are blessed with so much energy, as most people of your generation are, I implore you to use that energy to change the world. The influence that you exert either small or large, will bring about a better world. Keep in mind that even though this planet is 4.6 billion years old, our world is unfinished, and you can make a difference.

Gandhi said: "The difference between what we do and what we are capable of doing would suffice to solve most of the world's problems." So this essay is a call to action, to do something productive and life-changing to bring about positive transformation in the world. How to do this:

1. Recognize that you have gifts to offer the world that will position you for implementing change. You may have the gift of persuasion, of organization, of take-charge authority, of behind-the-scenes steadiness and encouragement. Whatever they are, these gifts cannot be ignored if you strive to change the world.

Know in your heart that you have what you need to succeed. My maternal grandmother, Grandma Harley, used the word "gumption." To her it meant taking on a project and following it through to a successful end. Gumption has a connotation of personal power beyond that of most people. It has a "Yes, I can!" attitude that guarantees success. Rachel, you have gumption!

And finally, because you have gifts, and all you need to succeed, it is important what you do with those gifts. Albert Einstein said that "the world is a dangerous place to live, not because of the people who are evil, but because of the people who don't do anything about it." And Harriet Beecher Stowe wrote that "the bitterest tears shed over graves are for words left unsaid and deeds left undone."

This world is unfinished, and you are called upon to do your part—in your time and your space—to create a better world.

2. Henry David Thoreau said, "Aim above morality**. Be not simply good; be good for something.**"

Rachel, THIS is the leap you take in order to change the world. You go beyond being good to doing good. You become a giving and productive contributor to our world society.

In the Greek language there are two words that are used often for the concept of good. *Agathos* refers to being good in character, upright and moral. *Kalos* refers to doing good things. A person can have *agathos* without having *kalos*; his goodness of character never translates into compassionate action.[18]

To be a person who is capable of changing the world, you need to employ both forms of goodness—morality and action. Your morality causes you to have a caring and compassionate heart, and your belief in action impels you to pursue causes that are worthy.

Remember Tolstoy's story, "The Death of Ivan Illych." A man on his deathbed reflects on his life, how he had done everything right, obeyed the rules, become a judge, married, had children, and is looked upon as a success. Yet, in his last hours, he wonders why he feels a failure. The answer is that it is not enough to keep the rules, to be respectable. What are you doing for the common good?

After becoming a famous novelist, Tolstoy himself decided that this was not enough, that he must speak out against the treatment of the Russian peasants, that he must write against war and militarism."[19] It's not enough to be good, you must be good for something.

3. Develop a world view. We are all brothers and sisters. Make your perspective global. Mothers in the Sudan love their children; mothers in Samoa love their children; mothers in Manhattan love their children. There is despair and hopelessness in the Sudan, in Samoa, in Manhattan. There is joy and encouragement in the Sudan, in Samoa, in Manhattan. We are a global community.

It is important that you sense the wholeness and meaning of life. And, yes, Rachel, you will discover the meaning of life. It will be personal and profound.

I hope that it encompasses some of the qualities that philosophers through the centuries have defined as essential to meaning: something that provides rewarding experiences to those affected, that overcomes challenges and improves the quality of life for others, that promotes friendship, beauty and knowledge, that causes the excellence of your humanity to shine, and that is positively oriented toward final value that transcends self.[20]

Though some people find meaning without believing in a Supreme Being, I hope YOU see all of humankind as created beings and that, therefore, there is a Creator. I hope you come to understand deep in your soul that our Creator God has a purpose for your life. And that this purpose is to change the world for the better. Then you will use your gifts, your insight, your love for humanity and your passion to accomplish remarkable things.

But some personal qualifications are necessary to bring about change:

Changing the world will take a lot of **patience**. In 1775 John Adams wrote in one of his many letters to his dear wife Abigail these worlds: "But America is a great, unwieldy Body. Its Progress must be slow. It is like a large Fleet sailing under Convoy. The fleetest Sailors must wait for the dullest and slowest. Like a Coach and six—the swiftest Horses must be slackened and the slowest quickened, that all may keep an even Pace."[21] So keep in mind that change requires patience.

Change also requires a **community of supporters**, a fellowship of like minds. Surround yourself with people of purpose, people who have thought through life's big issues and have concluded that they can and will pursue the grander ideals and causes that bring about a peaceful and better world.

And, Rachel, you will want to **prepare carefully** to make change in the world. Way back in 1670 in Canada, the Hudson Bay Company was founded. Its industry was fur trading, and this company was known for its preparation before trading journeys were undertaken.

On the first night the frontiersmen always camped only a few miles from headquarters. This gave them time to sort through supplies and check equipment. Then if anything was forgotten, they were only a short distance from camp and could return to get those forgotten, but needed, items.[22] This exacting preparation caused them to be greatly successful in their fur trading business. So it is in life, especially if your mission is to change the world.

Clarify your vision of what you can do to change the world. Your leadership for change will rise or fall on the scope of your vision.

"Vision is the first basic ingredient of leadership, the most pivotal of all the characteristics that outstanding leaders possess." (Warren Bennis)

Arm your vision with thorough knowledge of the cause which you espouse, and with that community of supporters who believe, like you, that change is possible, necessary and doable. When that happens, the world better watch out!

4. Take charge. A sentence I read thirty years ago has stayed with me and speaks to this concept of taking charge in order to make a difference in the world:

"God stores the hills with marble, but he never built a Parthenon; he fills the mountains with ore, but he never made a needle or locomotive."[23]

Rachel, it would be presumptuous of me to direct your path as you find causes to pursue in your efforts to change the world. But may I suggest some guidelines to employ in your pursuit:

1. **Look to the future.** Futurists talk of "trend analysis." That is a way of saying that we should study current trends to see where the world is headed so we can apply our influence where it will be most effective.

2. **Listen to the wise voices of the past.** Study the ways of Jesus, first of all, then the worlds' great philosophers. But don't neglect modern voices like those of Mahatma Gandhi and Martin Luther King, Jr. Their teachings and examples of non-violence changed the world.

3. **Do what you do with a loving heart**. Rabbi Harold Kushner said: "Do things for other people not because of who they are or what they do in return, but because of who you are."

4. Remember that **you may not see the results** of your efforts. It took many, many years to ratify the 19th Amendment giving women the right to vote. Untold numbers of women stood on the noble shoulders of others before them—those who did not live to see it happen, like Susan B. Anthony and Elizabeth Cady Stanton—but in 1920 this amendment was ratified.

5. **Speak up** when others make offensive remarks. If you do not, you give assent and encouragement to the offenders.

6. If your crowd—those with whom you spend your time—choose to go the way that is unworthy and uncaring—then compel yourself to **change directions** (and friends).

7. Doing one good deed that effects change in one person or changing empires from tyranny to triumph count the same in the grand scheme of life. **What you do really does make a difference.**

British statesman Edmund Burke "believed that each generation is a small part of a long chain of history. We serve as trustees for the wisdom of the ages and are obliged to pass it down, a little improved, to our descendants."[24]

Rachel, it is a grand thing to be involved in something that transcends your own life, that moves you with passion and leaves a mark on the world for generations to come.

I am only one,
But still I am one,
I cannot do everything,
But still I can do something;
And because I cannot do everything
I will not refuse to do the something
I can do.

>   – Edward Everett Hale

"The difference between what we do and what we are capable of doing would suffice to solve most of the world's problems."
– Mahatma Gandhi

A FINAL THOUGHT

Well, Rachel, I've come to the end of these essays and there's one last family story I'd like to tell you. When you were six or seven years old, Granddad and I took you to our church. We had a new pastor and, as we were leaving the service and walking to the car, Granddad asked you what you thought of our new pastor. You said matter-of-factly, "He could use some more color."

Granddad asked what you meant by that, and you said: "He's not very exciting." Then you said thoughtfully, "You know, it's important to make the things that are true exciting, 'cause the things that aren't true are always exciting."

From then on those comments have been called The Rachel Principle in our family:

"It's important to make the things that are true exciting . . ."

Remember in my first comments I referred to your creating your own tapestry. Tapestry means "pictures or designs formed by threads." Your life pictures or designs will be of your own creation—you are "making" yourself right now—because of who you are and what your values are. Make it true and then your life will be exciting!

As you've matured and stand on the threshold of life, now graduating from college, two of your gifts have emerged and wrapped themselves around your heart: the gifts of dance and song writing. How talented you are in these areas!

There's a song that seems to sum up the things I've said in these essays: look for wonder, believe in yourself, learn from your mistakes, love unconditionally, and change the world. So I close with these words written by Mark D. Sanders and Tia Sillers and recorded by Lee Ann Womack:

I hope your never lose your sense of wonder
You get your fill to eat
But always keep the hunger.
May you never take one single breath for granted.
God forbid love ever leave you empty handed.

48

I hope you still feel small
When you stand by the ocean.

Whenever one door closes,
I hope one more opens.
Promise me you'll give faith a fighting chance.
And when you get the choice to sit it out or dance,
I hope you dance,
I hope you dance.

I hope you never fear those mountains in the distance.
Never settle for the path of least resistance.
Living might mean taking chances
But they're worth taking.
Lovin' might be a mistake
But it's worth making.
Don't let some hell bent heart
Leave you bitter.
When you come close to selling out
Reconsider.
Give the heavens above
More than just a passing glance.

And when you get the choice to sit it out or dance,
I hope you dance,
I hope you dance.[25]

One last thing, Rachel: KNOW HOW MUCH I LOVE YOU . . .

NOTES

1. Robert Fulghum, *Uh-Oh* (New York: Villard Books, 1991), p 31.

2. Dick Capen in *The Transparent Leader* by Dwight L. Johnson (Eugene, OR: Harvest House, 2001), pp. 161-163.

3. Arthur Gordon, "Open Windows to Wonder," *Guideposts,* December 1993, p. 41.

4. "A More Joyful Life," *Parade, Magazine*, October 15, 2000, p. 7.

5. *The Book of Abigail and John, Selected Letters of the Adams Family*, edited by L. H. Butterfield, Marc Friedlaender and Mary-Jo Kline (Cambridge, Massachusetts and London, England: Harvard University Press, 1975), p. 8.

6. Gareth Cook, Chattanooga *Times Free Press*, June, 11, 2011, p. B7.

7. King Duncan, *The Amazing Law of Influence* (Gretna, LA: Pelican Publishing Company, 2001), p. 120.

8. Elizabeth Sherrill, "The Not-So-Ugly Duckling," *Guideposts*, January, 2006, pp. 26-27, originally from National Public Radio, *Sound & Spirit*, host, Ellen Kushner.

9. Wayne Brouwer, *Sermons by Wayne Brouwer*, "The Courage to Live" (Seven Worlds Corporation, 1999), p. 15.

10. Mary Pickford, *The Quotable Woman* (Philadelphia: Running Press, 1991), p. 137.

11. Reprinted in a Dear Abby column, February 10, 1998.

12. Rona Barrett, *The Quotable Woman* (Philadelphia: Running Press, 1991), p. 93.

13. This poem, written by Kent Keith and paraphrased by Mother Teresa, is engraved on the wall of her Home for Children in Calcutta.

14. Norman Wright, *Real Solutions for Overcoming Discouragement, Rejection, and the Blues* (Ann Arbor: H. Servant Publishing, 2001).

15. Maxie D. Dunnam, *The Christian Way* (Grand Rapids: Frances Asbury Press, 1984).

16. Madeleine L'Engle, *Sold Into Egypt* (Wheaton, IL: Harold Shaw Publishers, 1989), p. 70.

17. Sidney Poitier, *AARP* magazine, September & October 2008, p. 118.

18. Joseph M. Stowell, *The Trouble With Jesus* (Chicago: Moody Publishers, 2003), pp. 95-101.

19. Dr. Howard Zinn, addressing graduates of Spelman College, May 2005, in The Rev. Dr. Gary Charles, Day 1, 2005. http://www.day1.net/index. php5 ?view=transcripts&tid=5 12.

20. Metz, Thaddeus, "The Meaning of Life," *The Stanford Encyclopedia of Philosophy (Fall 2008 Edition)*, Edward N. Zalta (ed.), URL = <http://plato.stanford. Edu/archives /fall2008/entries/life-meaning/>.

21. Butterfield, Friedlaender, Kline, p. 89.

22. Fulghum, pp. 25-26.

23 Harry Emerson Fosdick, *The Meaning of Prayer* (New York: Association Press, 1934), p. 64.

24. David Brooks, "Theories of Change," Chattanooga *Times Free Press*, May 30, 2010.

25. (c) 2000 Sony/ATV Music Publishing LLC, Choice Is Tragic Music, MCA, and Soda Creek Songs. All rights on behalf of Sony/ATV Music Publishing LLC and Choice Is Tragic Music administered by Sony/ATV Music Publishing LLC, 8 Music Square West, Nashville, TN 37203. All rights reserved. Used by permission.

For more Seven Worlds Books please got to
www.sevenworldspub.com

SEVEN WORLDS PUBLISHING

www.ingramcontent.com/pod-product-compliance
Lightning Source LLC
Chambersburg PA
CBHW060614030426
42337CB00018B/3060

* 9 7 8 0 9 3 6 4 9 7 6 3 1 *